BEAUTIFUL,

BE-YOU-TIFUL

YOU

MILA FOX

BEAUTIFUL,
BE-YOU-TIFUL
YOU

BY MILA FOX

WRITTEN BY MILA FOX

ILLUSTRATED BY MILA FOX

EDITED BY BEATRIZ FOX

COPYRIGHT © 2018 BY MILA FOX

ALL RIGHTS RESERVED.

10 9 8 7 6 5 4 3 2

MEANT 2 BEA PUBLICATIONS
PROVIDENCE, RHODE ISLAND

MORE BY THIS AUTHOR

BARE TO THE BONES: CHARCOAL FIGURE ART
BE-YOU-TIFUL CRUSADE: LEND A HAND
BE-YOU-TIFUL CRUSADE: DON'T BE AFRAID
BE-YOU-TIFUL CRUSADE: BULLYING CAN HAPPEN AT ANY AGE
BE-YOU-TIFUL CRUSADE: SIBLINGS DAY
CHIC-IPEDIA

to anyone who has ever doubted themselves or their place in this world

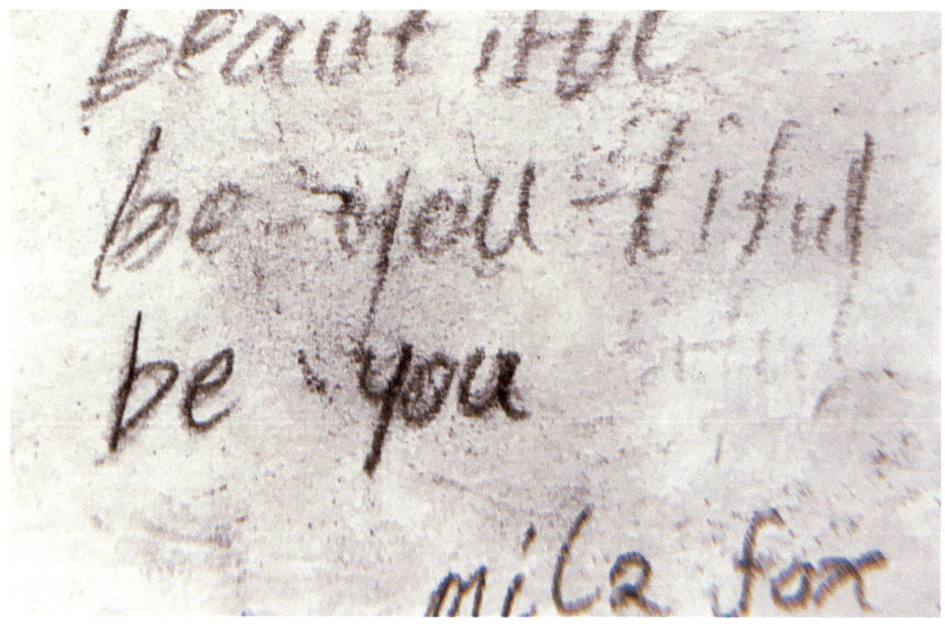

this is for you

"love yourself":

to start
to start

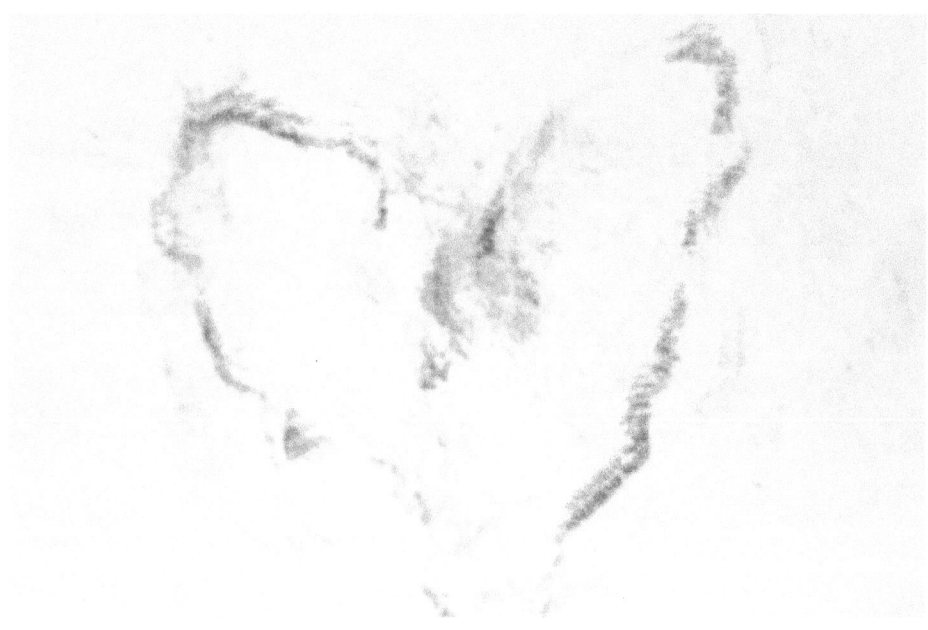

you are
you are be=you=tiful

no matter what your skin tone, body configuration, sexuality, or beliefs

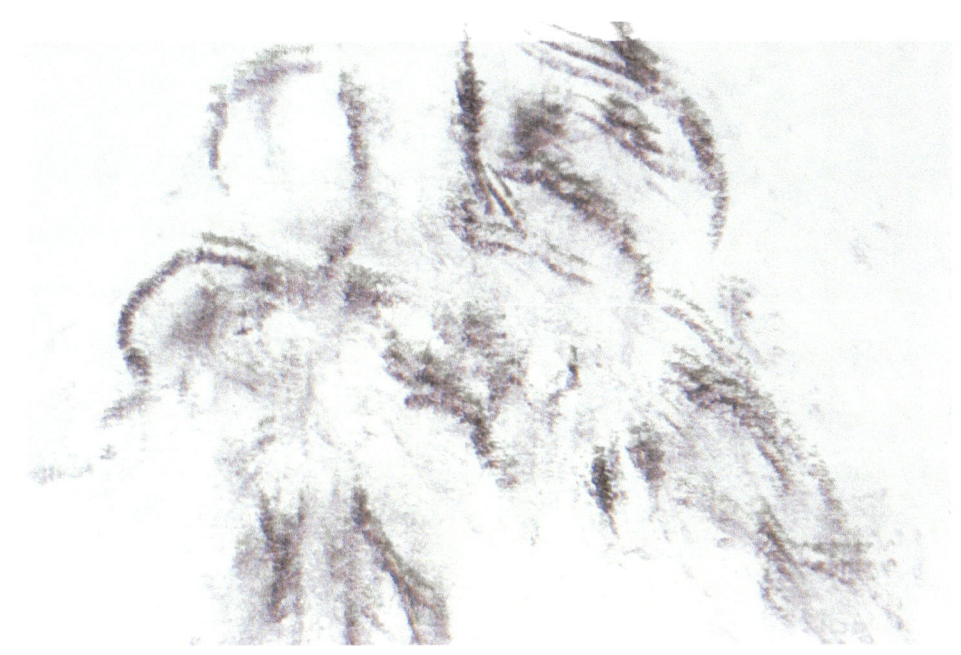

you are important

the world wasn't designed for a single "look"

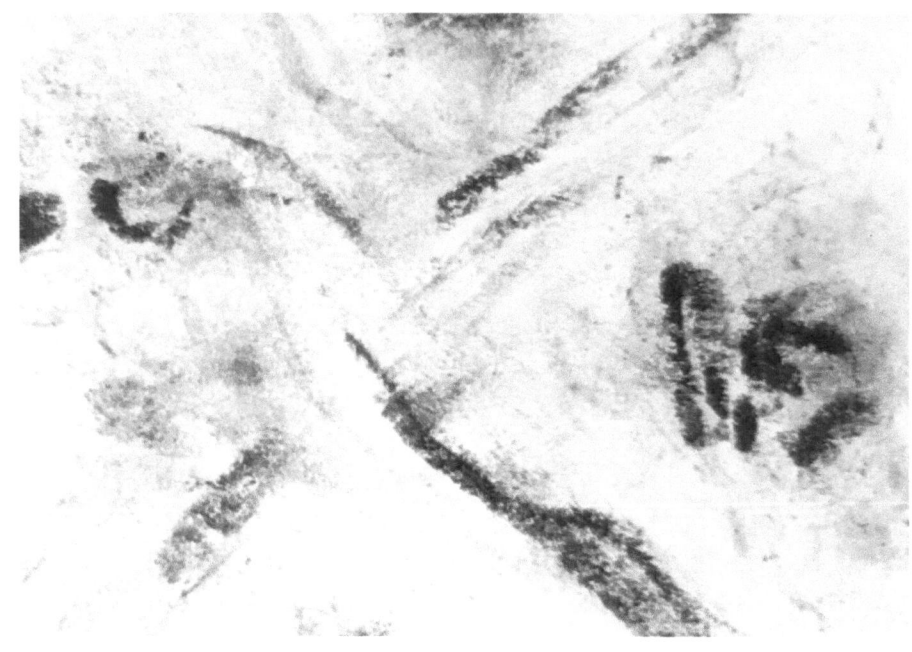

diversity is what makes the world more colorful...

people often say that you have to love yourself before you can love anyone else

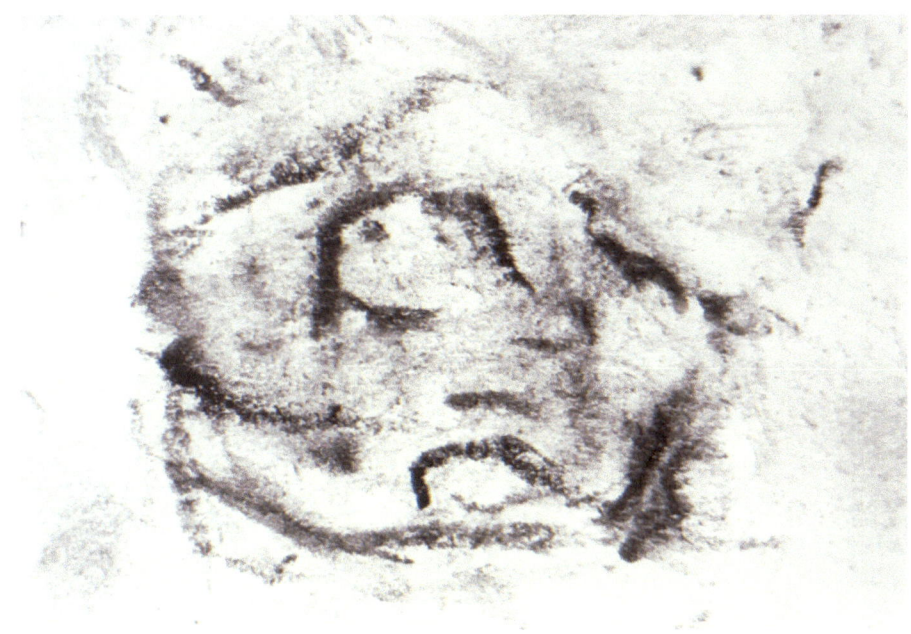

I think that's true
I think that's true

because, in one way or another someone will let you down in life

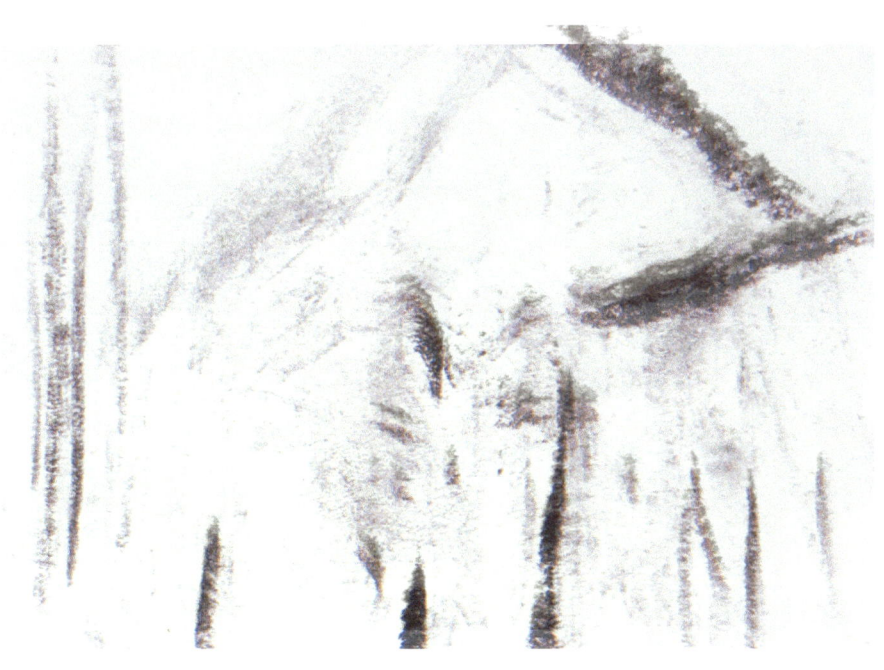

maybe even break your heart

in those situations, the most important thing is for you to be able to pick yourself up

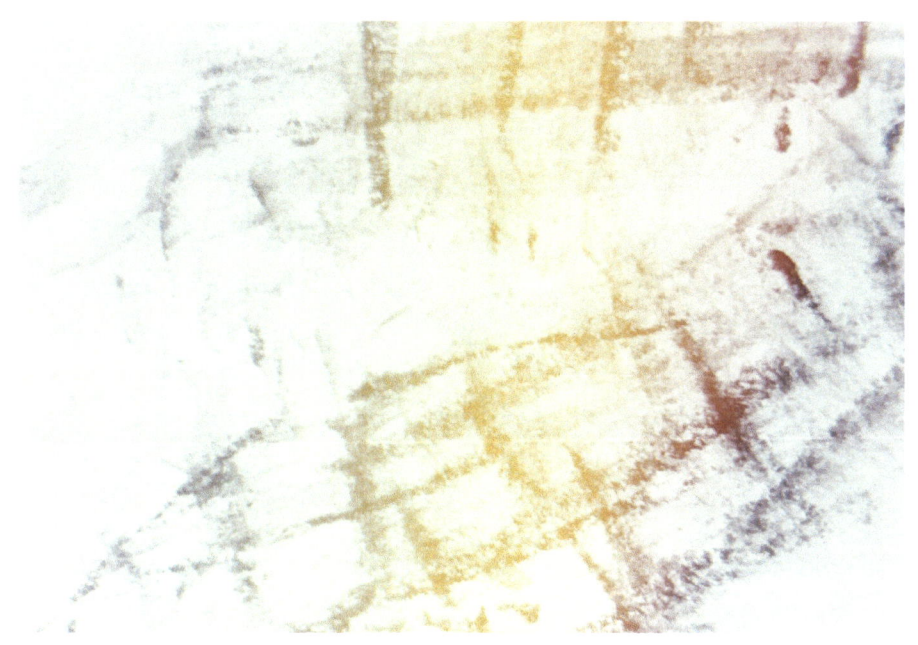

you <u>need</u> to pick yourself up

your mind, body, and soul are worth far more than you could ever imagine

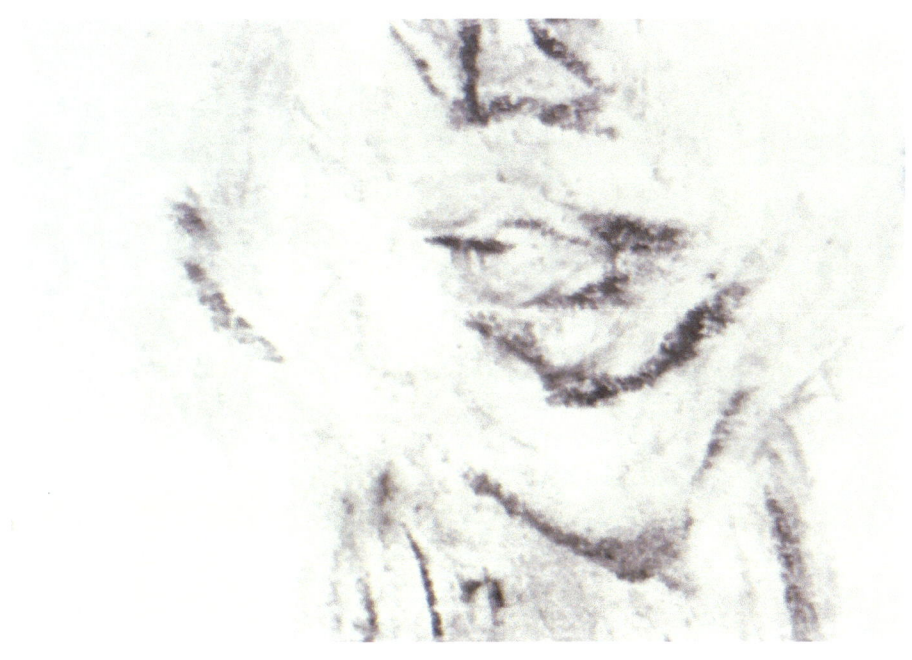

NOBODY DESERVES TO
HAVE THE POWER TO
TAKE THOSE AWAY
FROM YOU

"the 'yellow brick road' is overrated":

live a life full of laughter and happiness

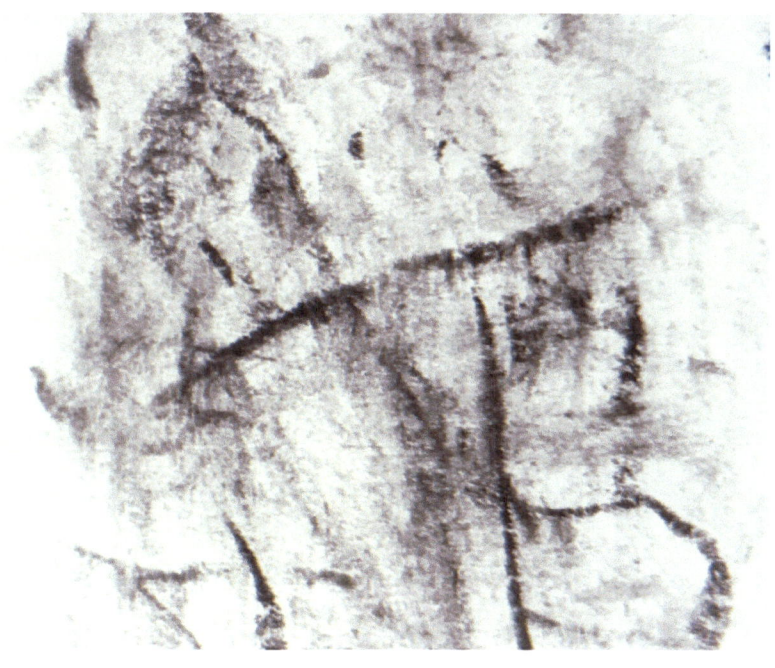

chase your wildest dreams

don't waste time chasing "Plan B"

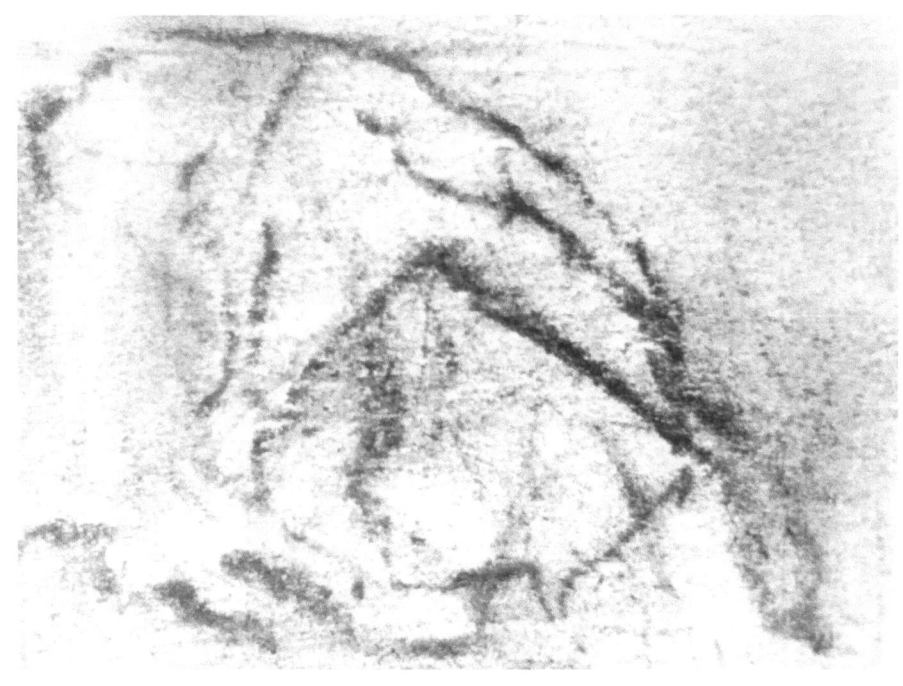

if "Plan A" is what makes you beam

life often presents us with a series of paths,

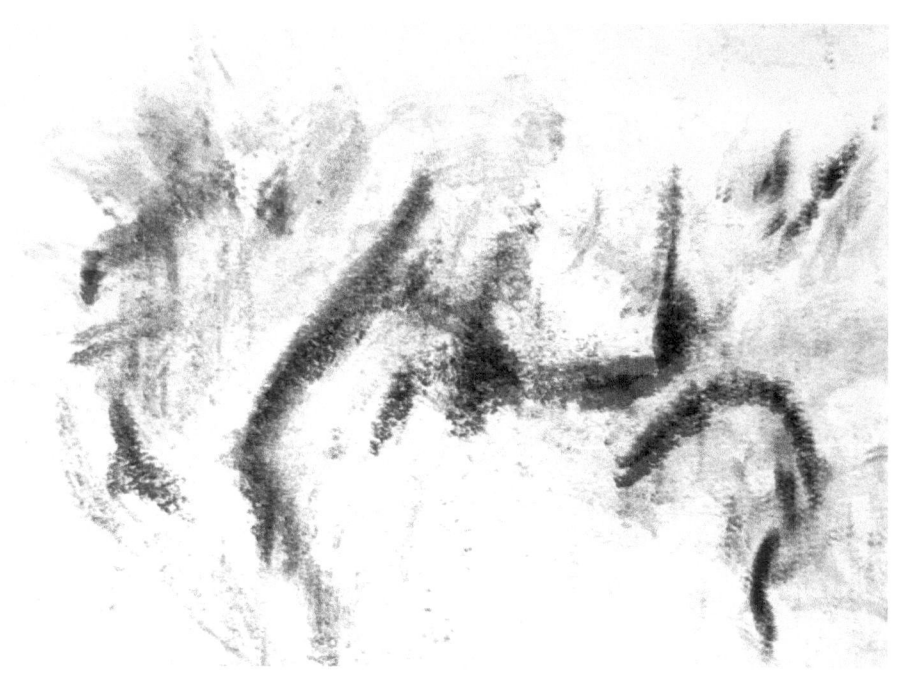

and many choose the "yellow brick road"

~~frankly, I think it's overrated~~ frankly, I think it's overrated...

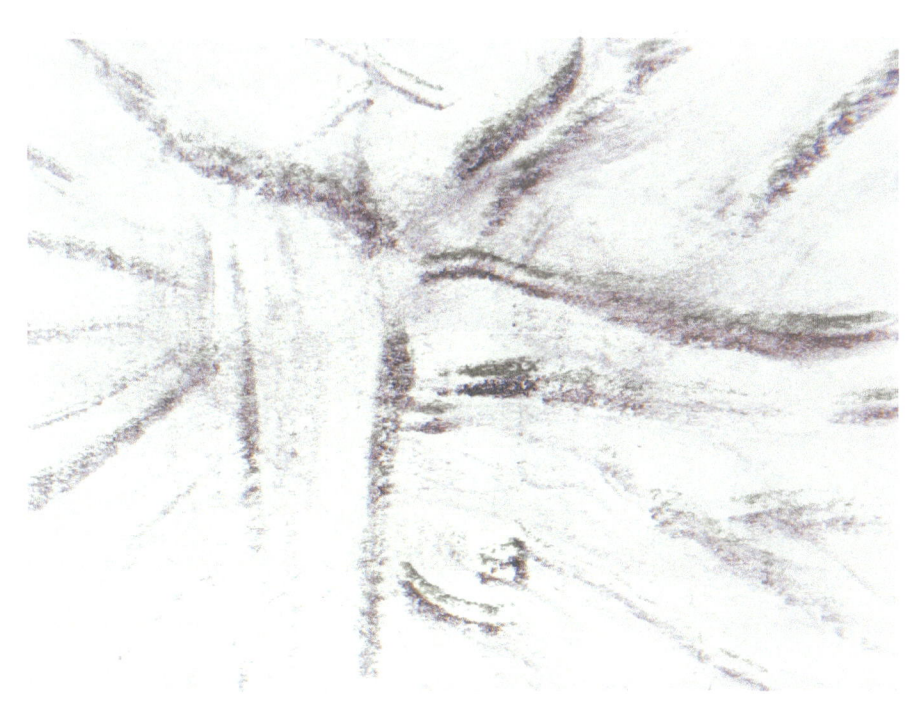

many wonder why they're unhappy after they've chosen
the infamous path towards success

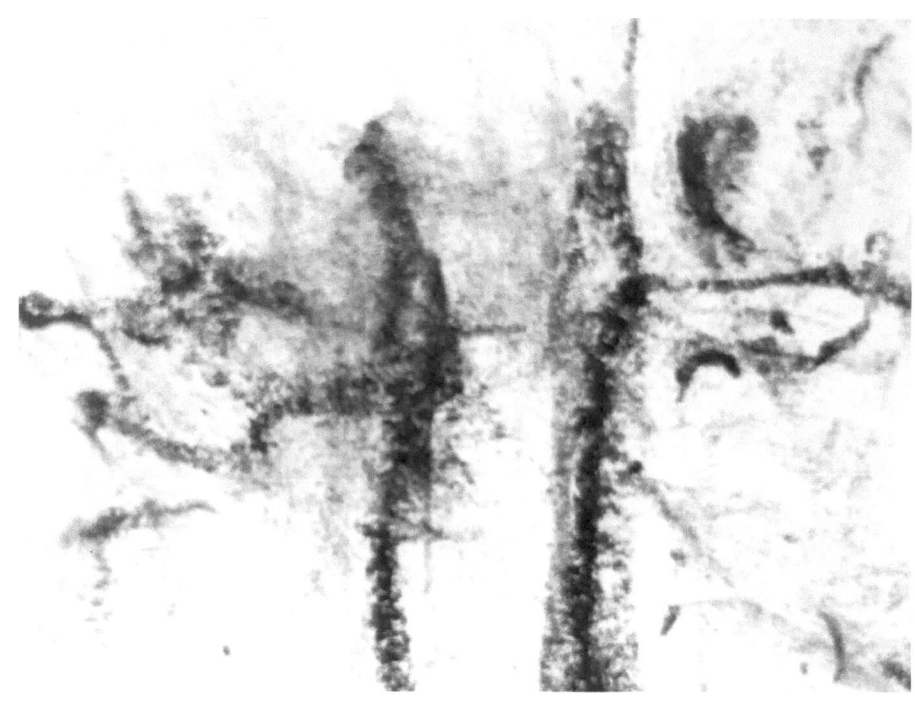

but there lies the problem of it all

we are all individuals!

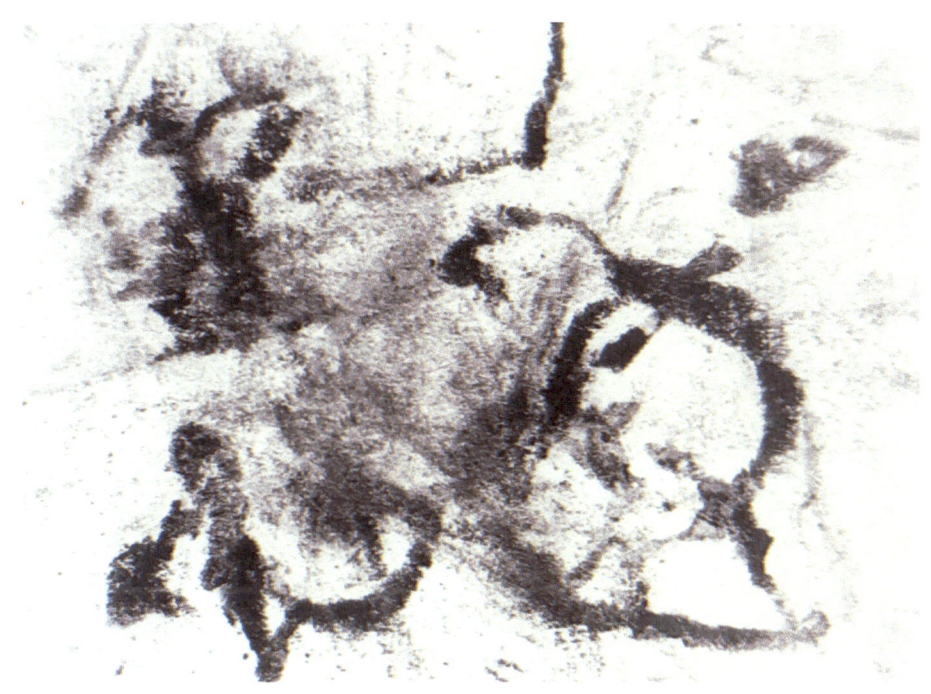

each one of us destined for a different path in life

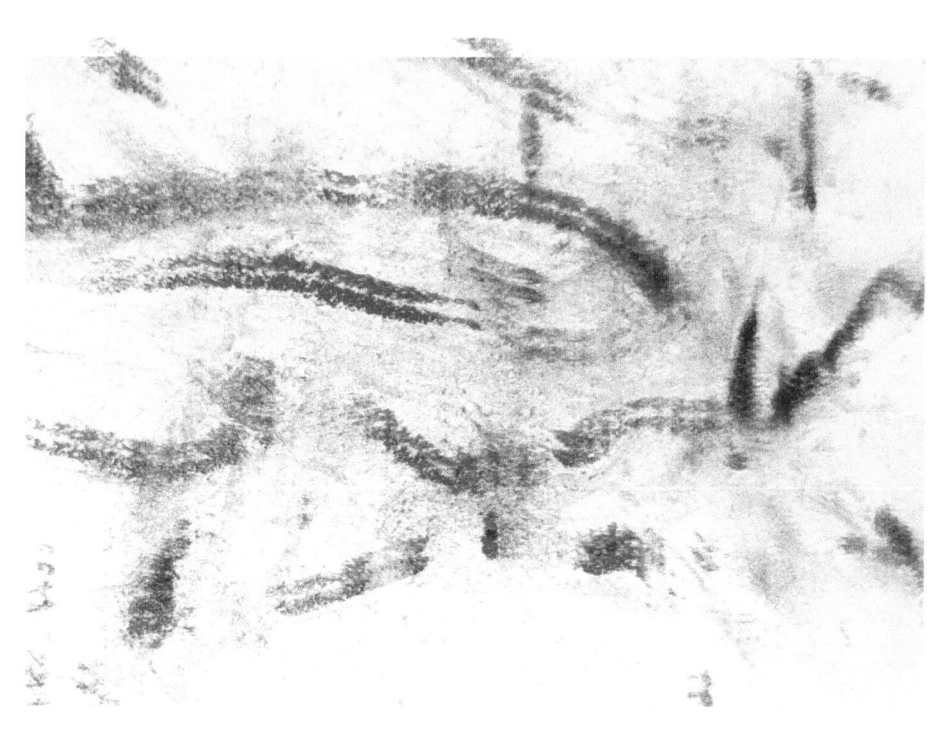

so, take the path that makes your heart full with excitement

it may look different

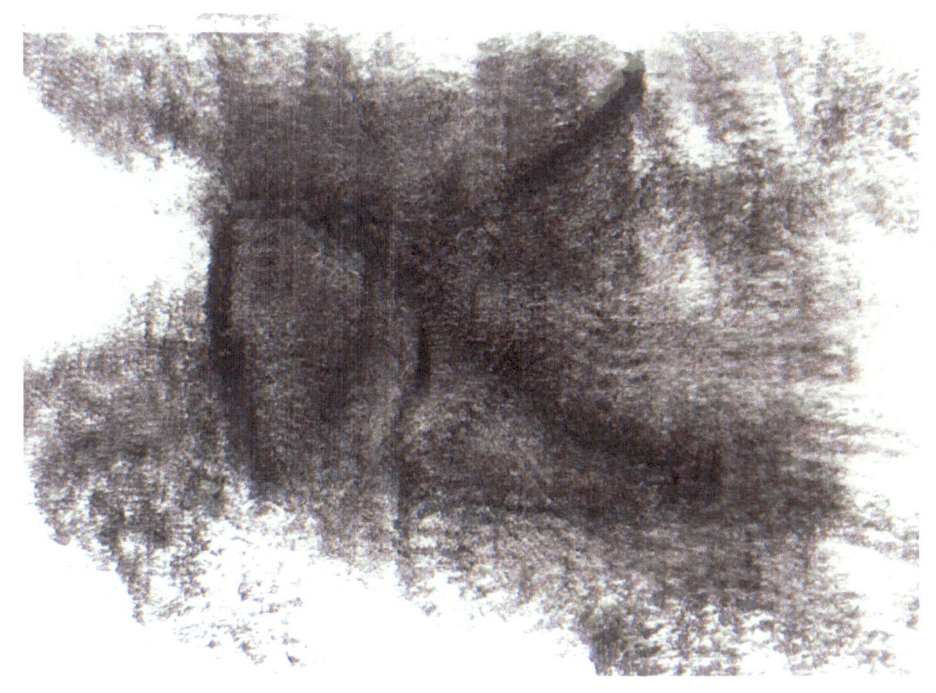

it may seem scary
it may seem scary

people might even make fun of you, assuming you're foolish...

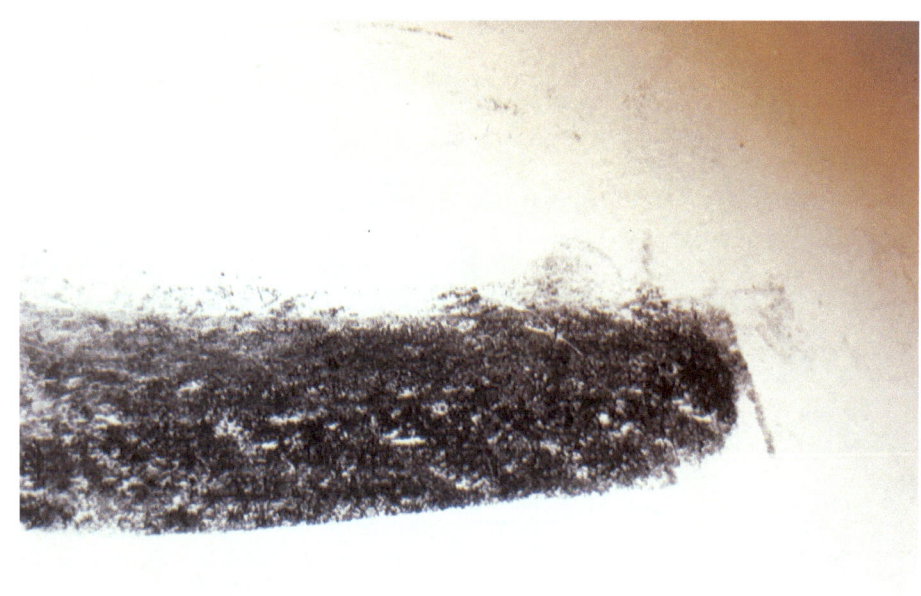

believing you're making a mistake

but, that's okay

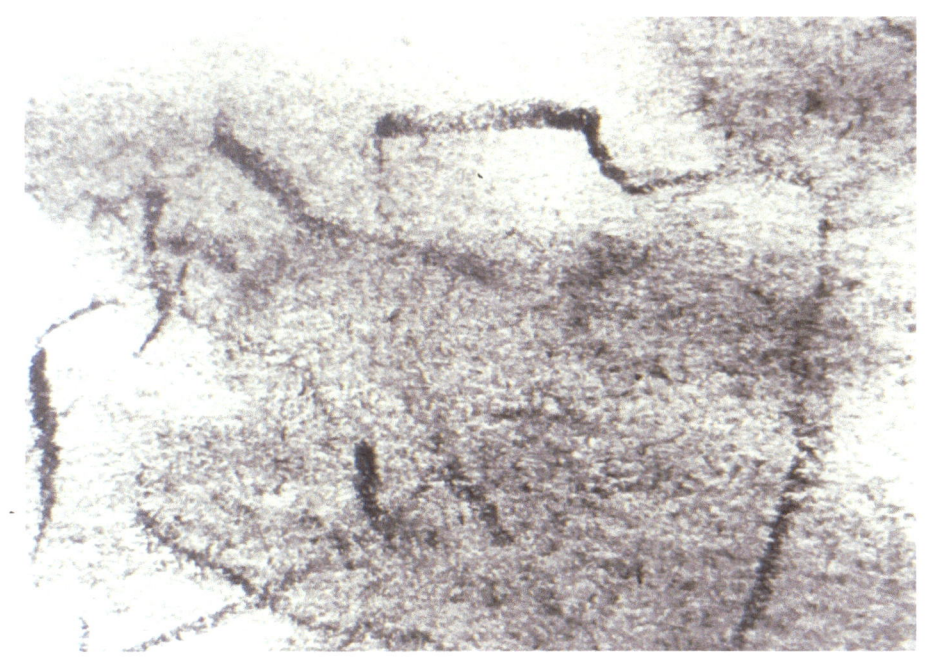

as long as you believe in yourself

NOTHING ELSE TRULY MATTERS

"every woman/man for themselves":
"every woman/man for themselves":

peer pressure comes in many shapes and sizes

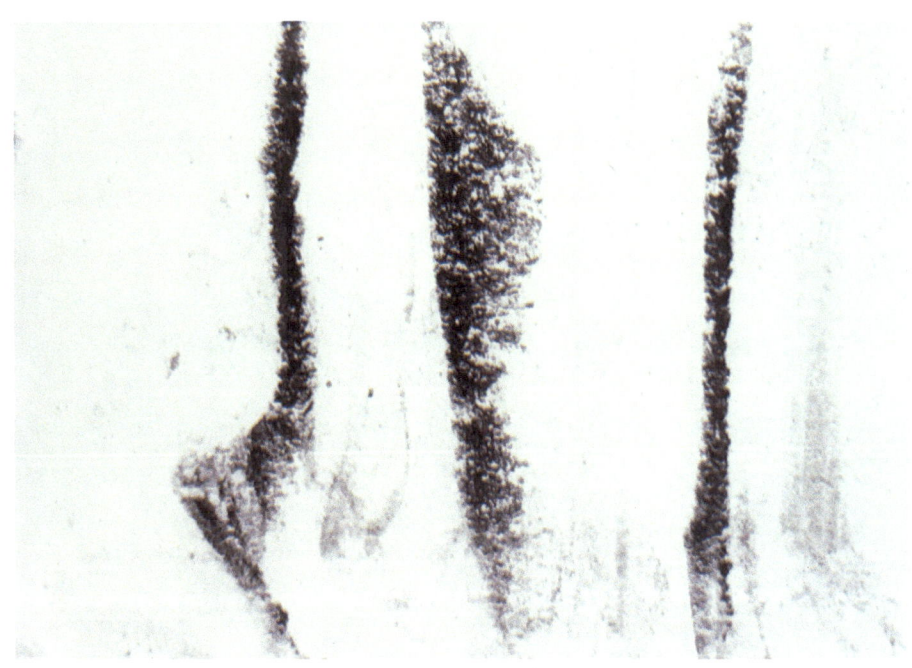

we never know when it's coming

so, if intimidation ever creeps upon you

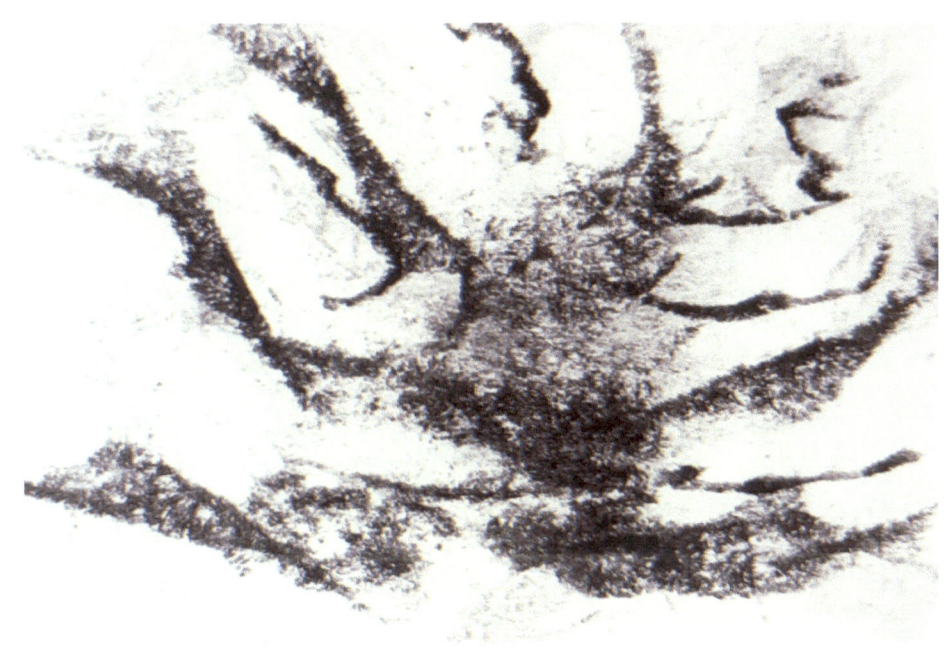

like a spider in the night

ask yourself this:

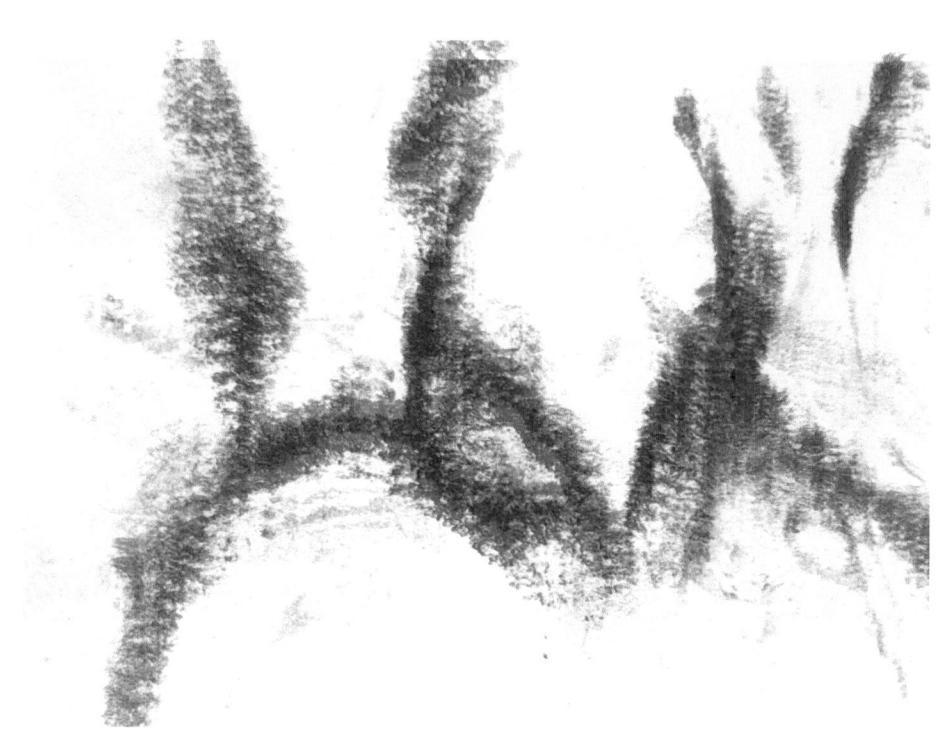

who will be there to pick you up if you fall?

for that, my friend, is the trick of it all:::

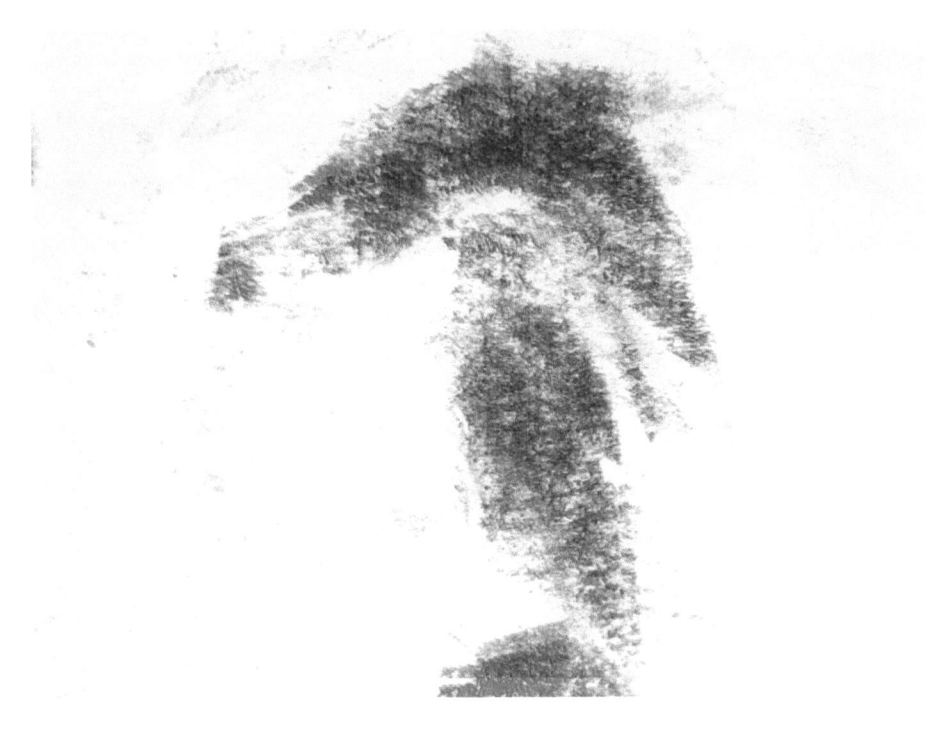

we're each in a "race" towards success
we're each in a "race" towards success

all of us trying to be the best

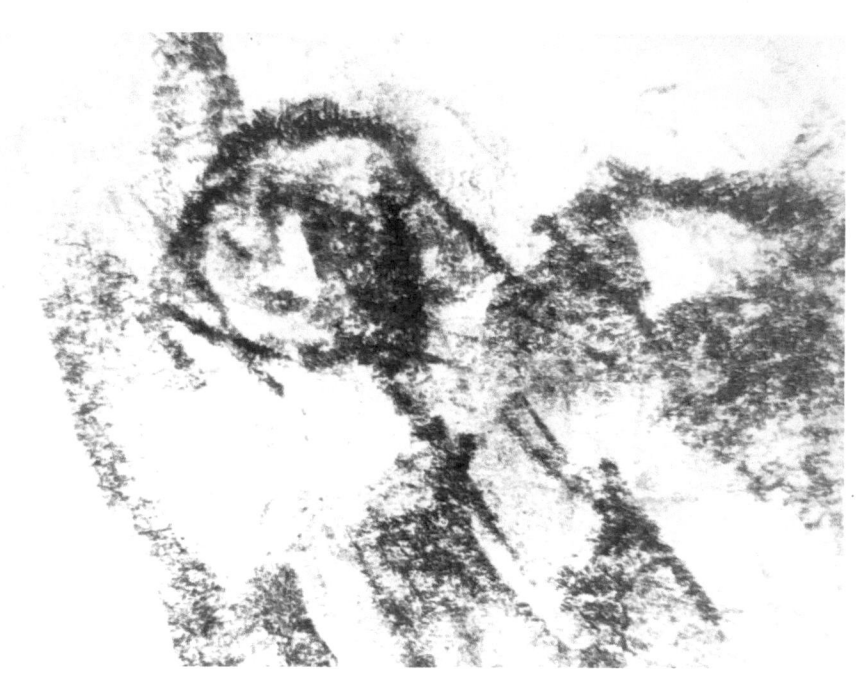

life is but a mountain that challenges us to climb to the top

there will be some who feel weak

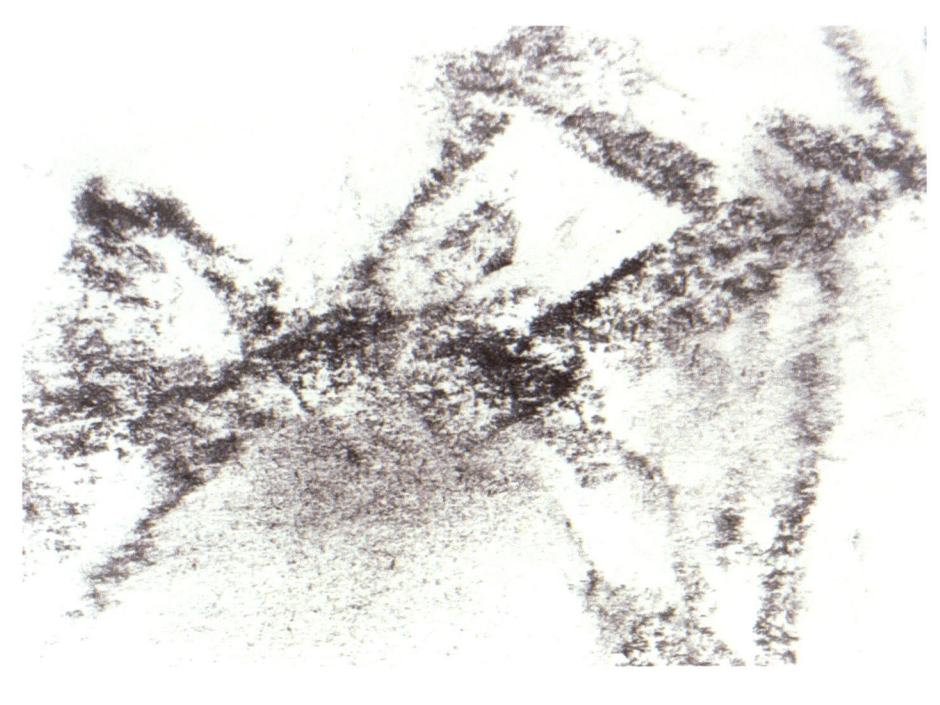

and those who feel intimidated will argue that it's you

they will try to slow you down or push you

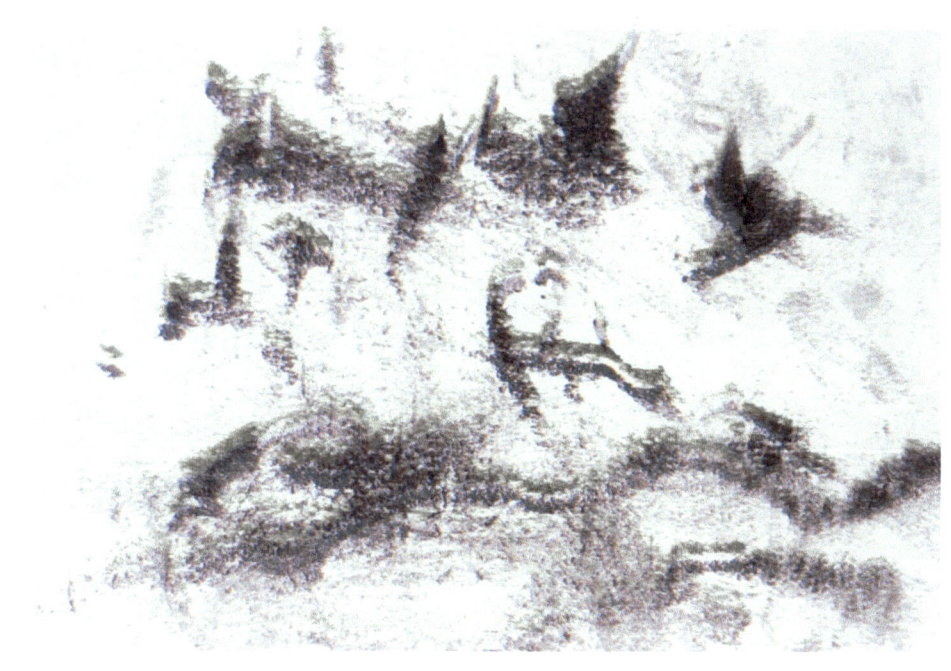

in an effort to make you fall

at the first sign of this = run

we all have far too many obstacles already
we all have far too many obstacles already

do what makes YOUR heart full with excitement

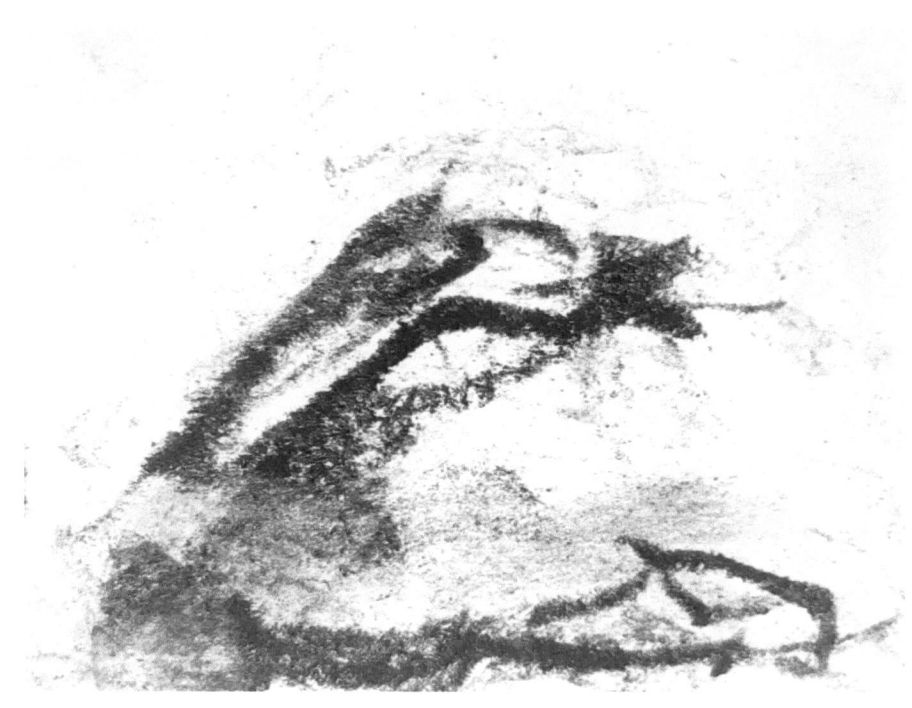

hold yourself to your values

and, if you do

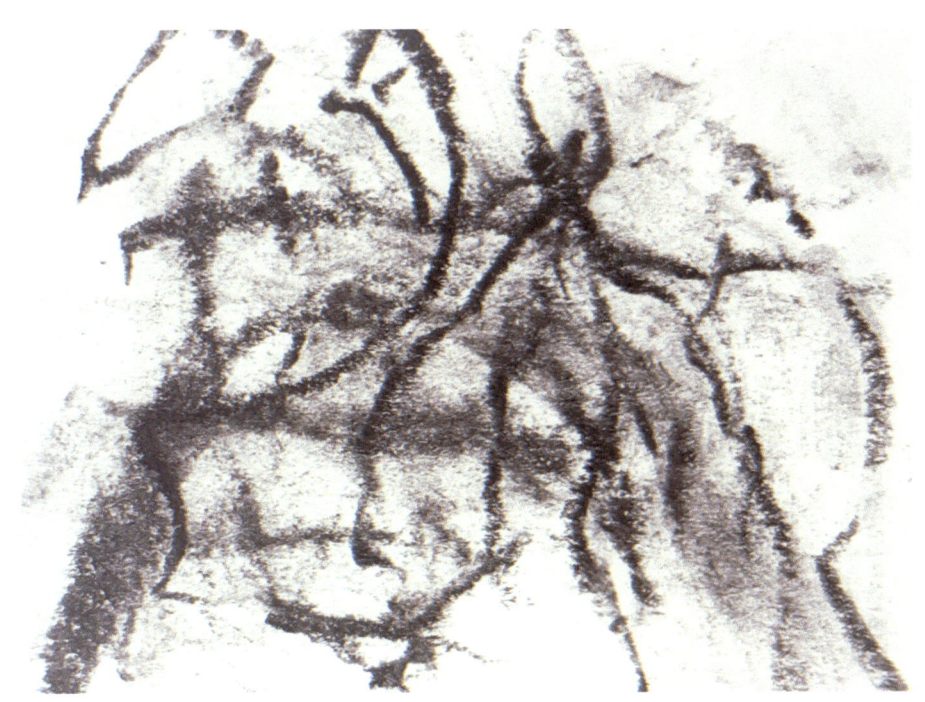

well... guess what?

YOU'VE ALREADY WON

"you are everything"
you are everything

Dear friend,

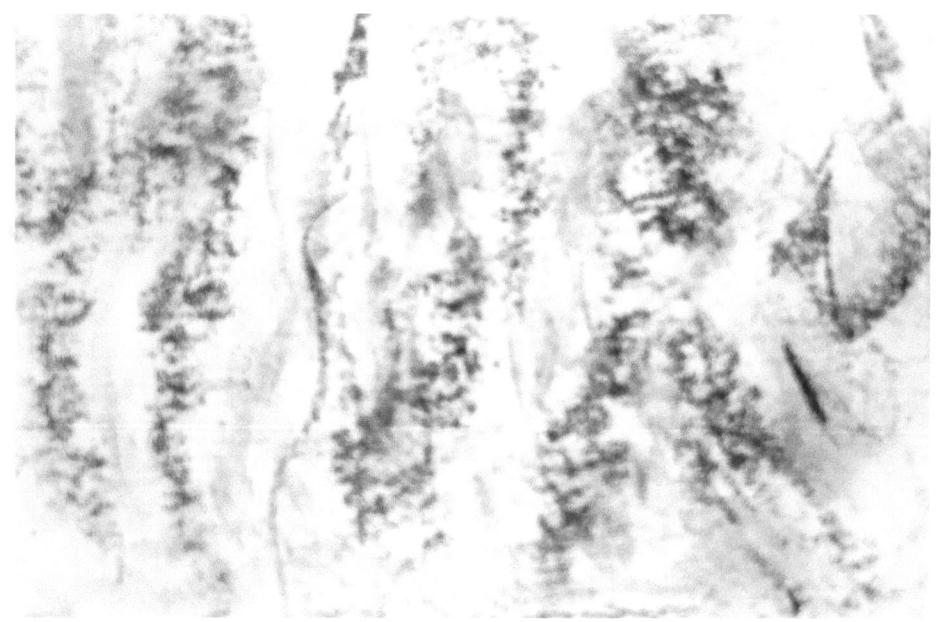

you are the pencil

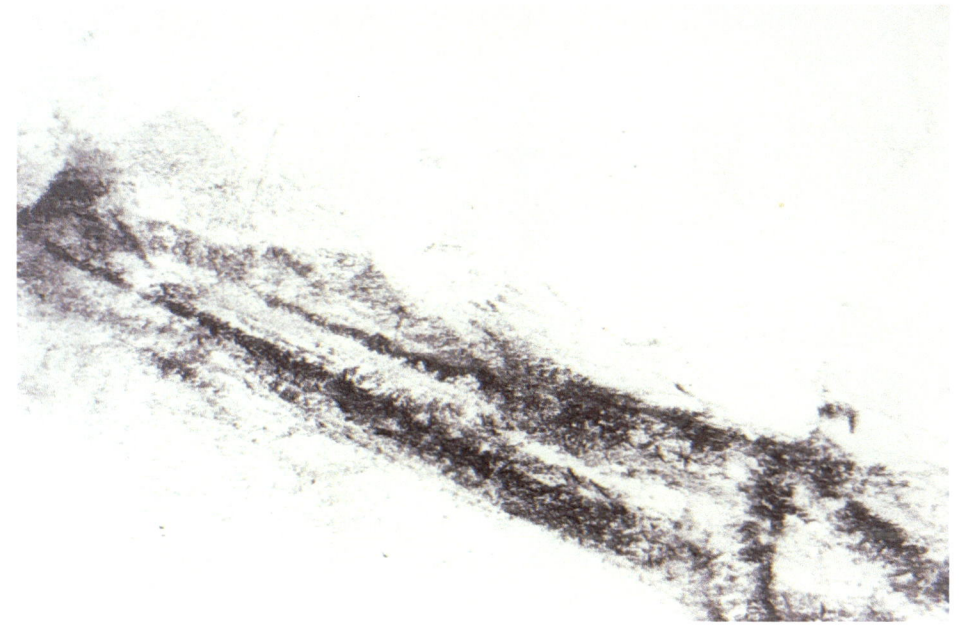

the paper

the paintbrush
the paintbrush

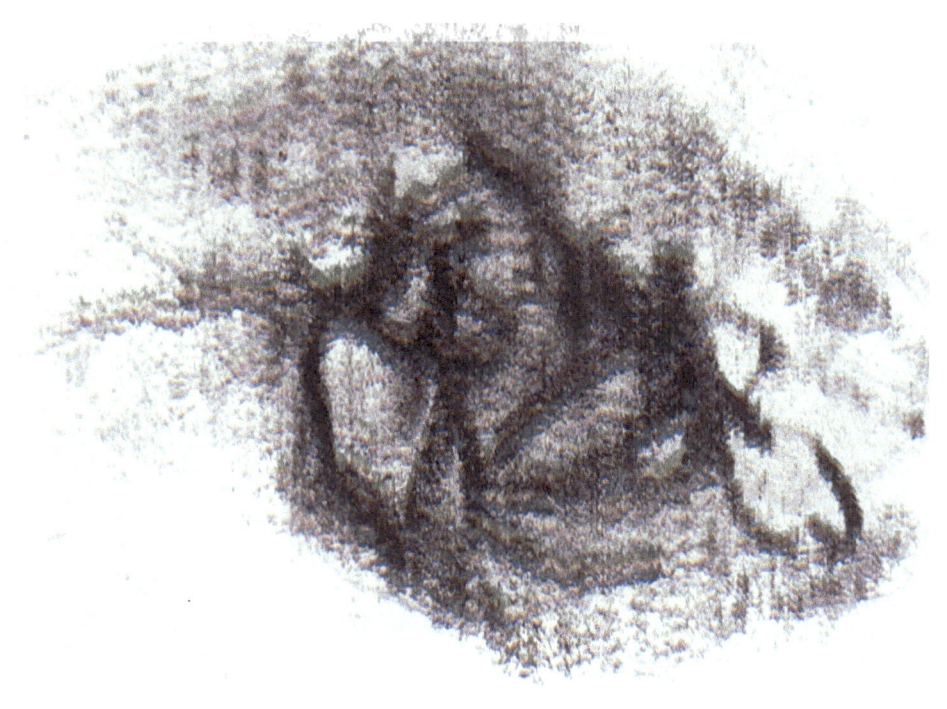

and the canvas

48

you are the narrator of your own story, however you
choose to tell it

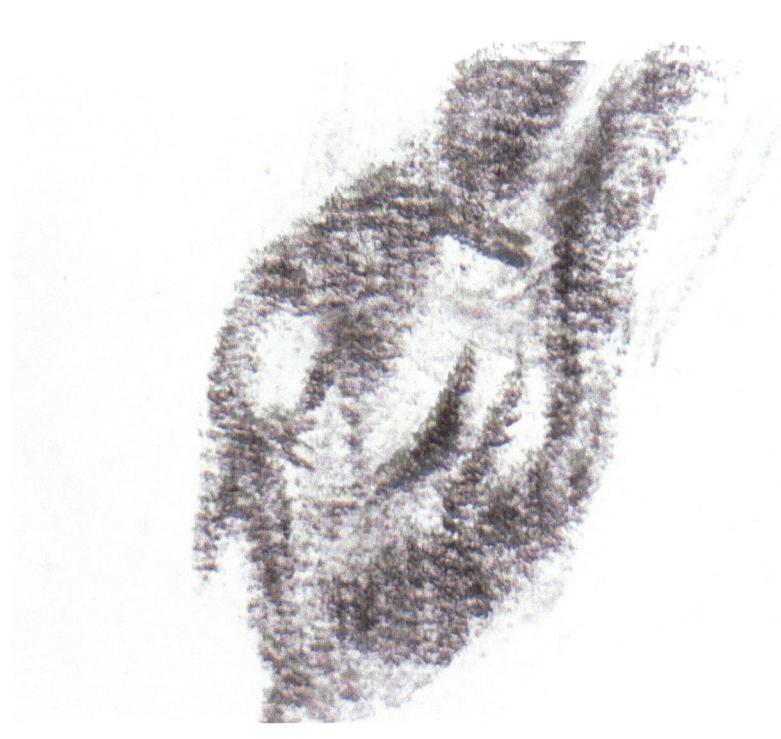

so get to work
so get to work

and please

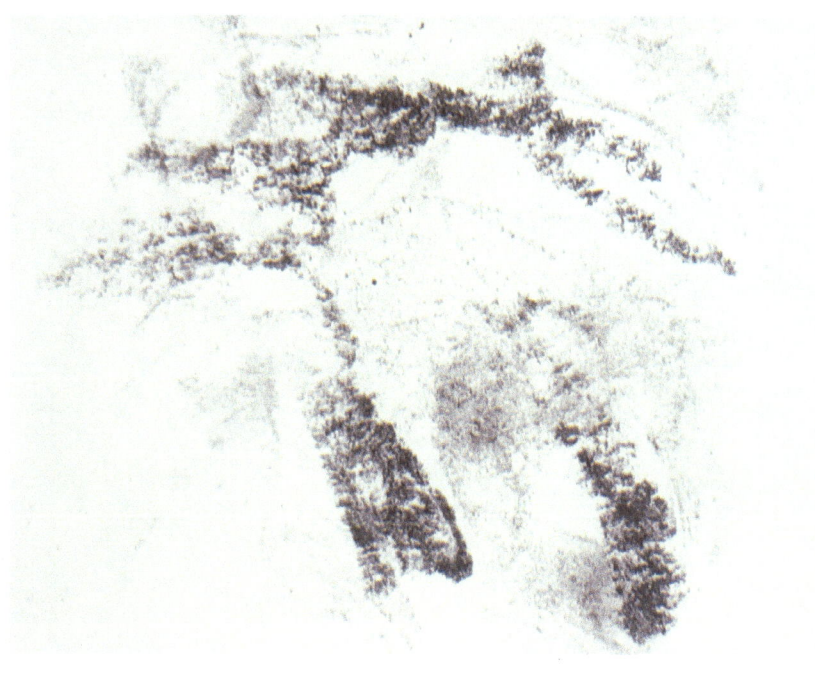

make it your own

don't veer away from your own path, hoping to follow someone else's

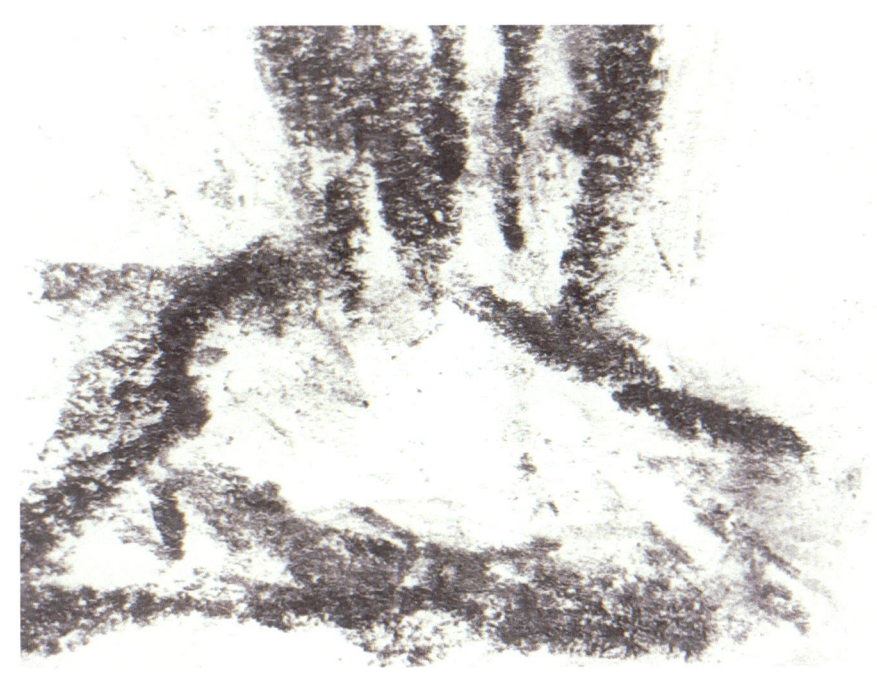

because, in the end

no one likes to read the same story
no one likes to read the same story

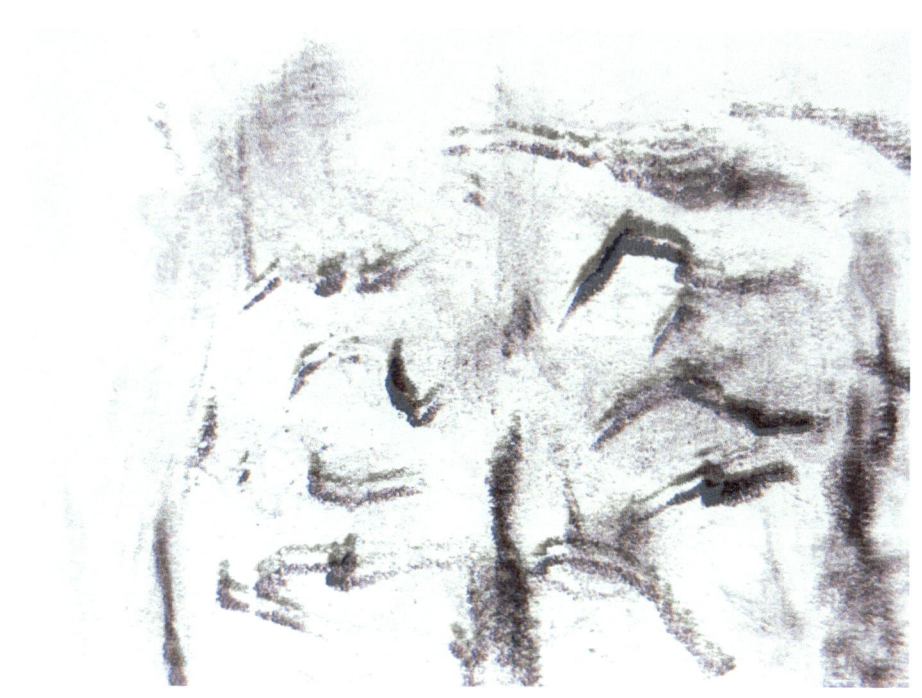

MAKE IT YOURS
and make it count
and make it count

"beautiful/be-you-tiful you":

along with the many beautiful things in life, is the presence of doubt

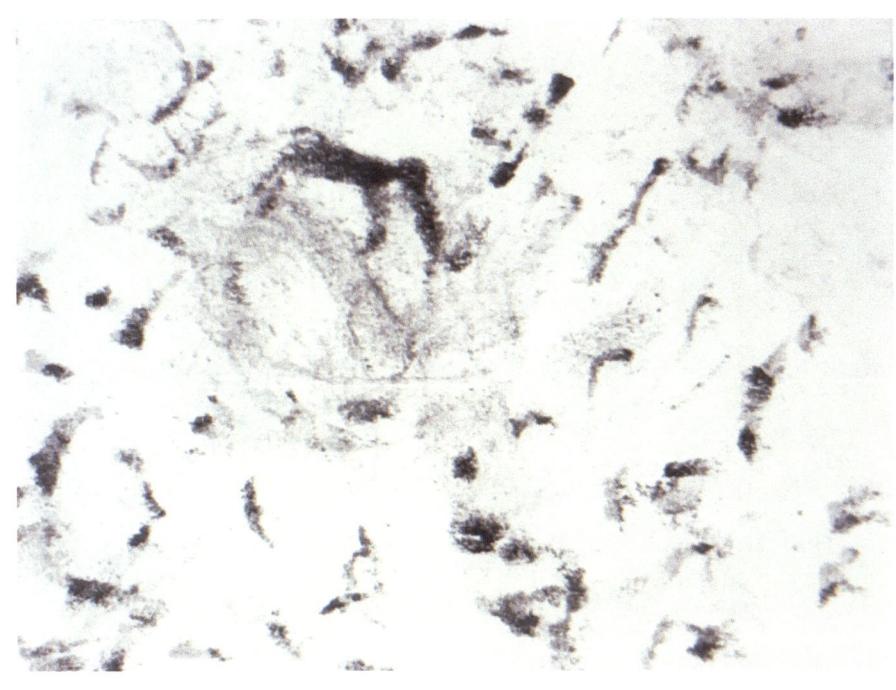

we're all in a constant battle with the negative voices in our head but think of it this way:

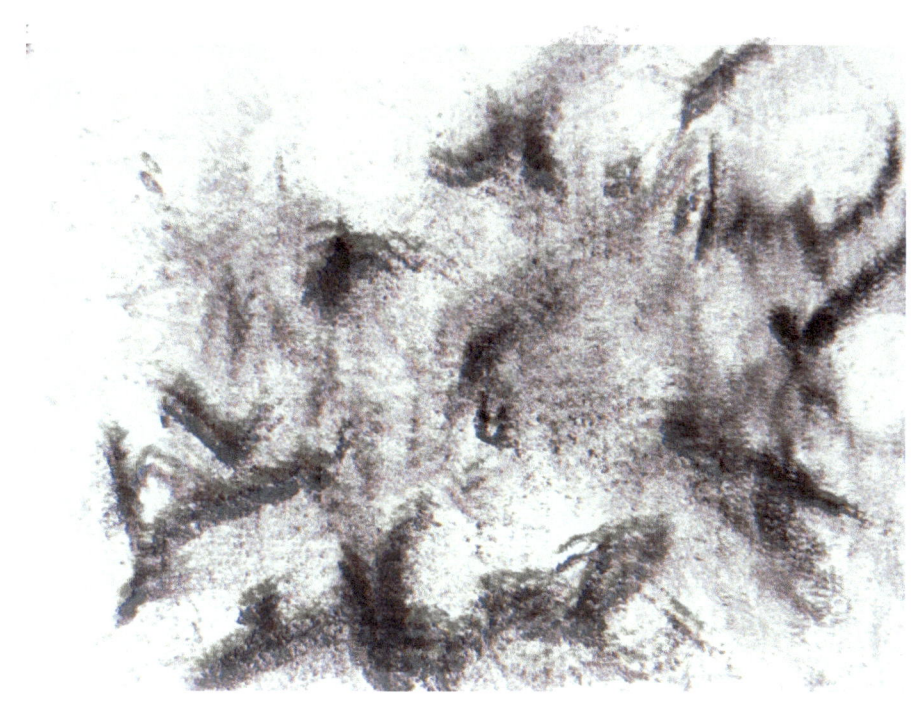

you are water and negativity is ice

§8

there cannot be one without the other

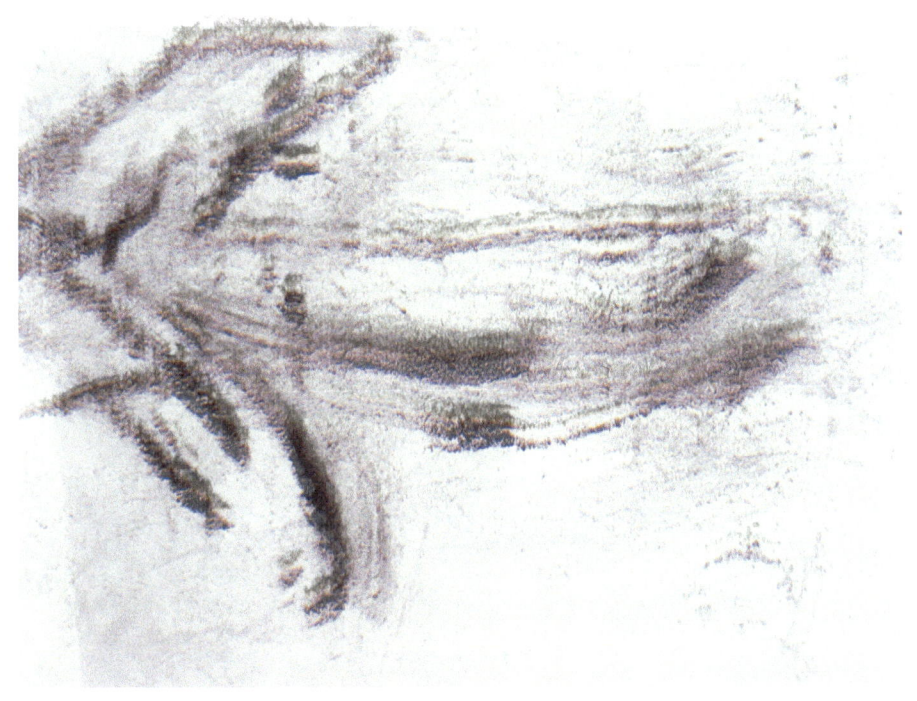

but you are in control

for, ice is a merely a form of water

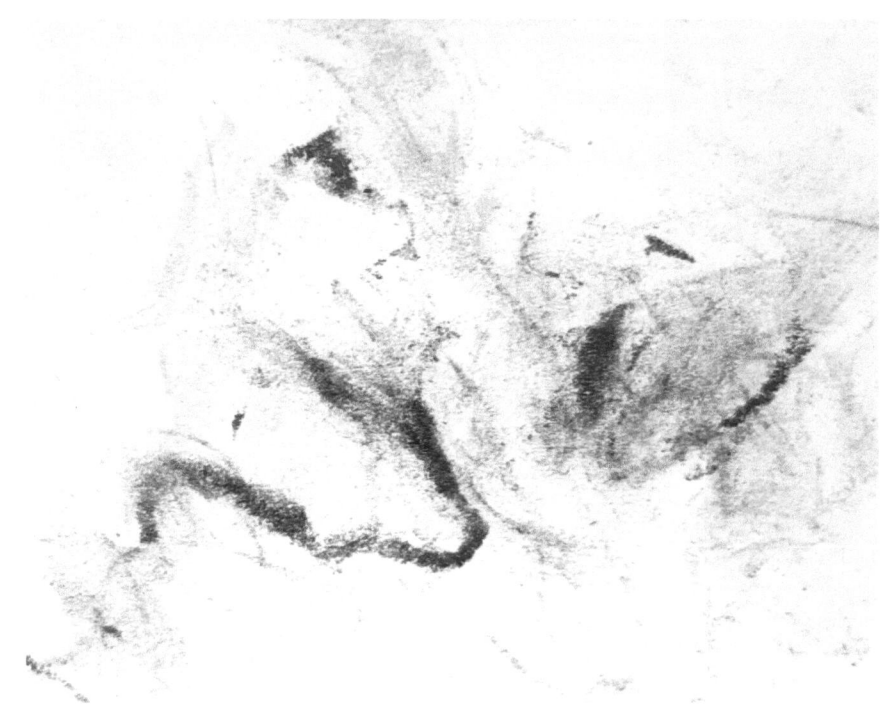

so whatever ignites your mind with happiness

set it on FIRE

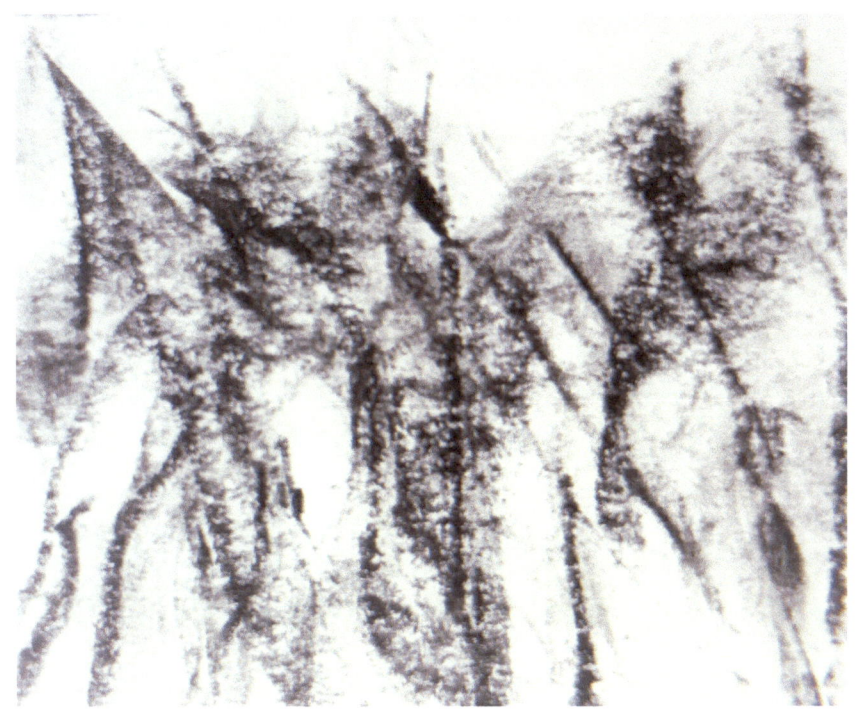

and destroy the extinguisher

because you are be-you-tiful
because you are be-you-tiful

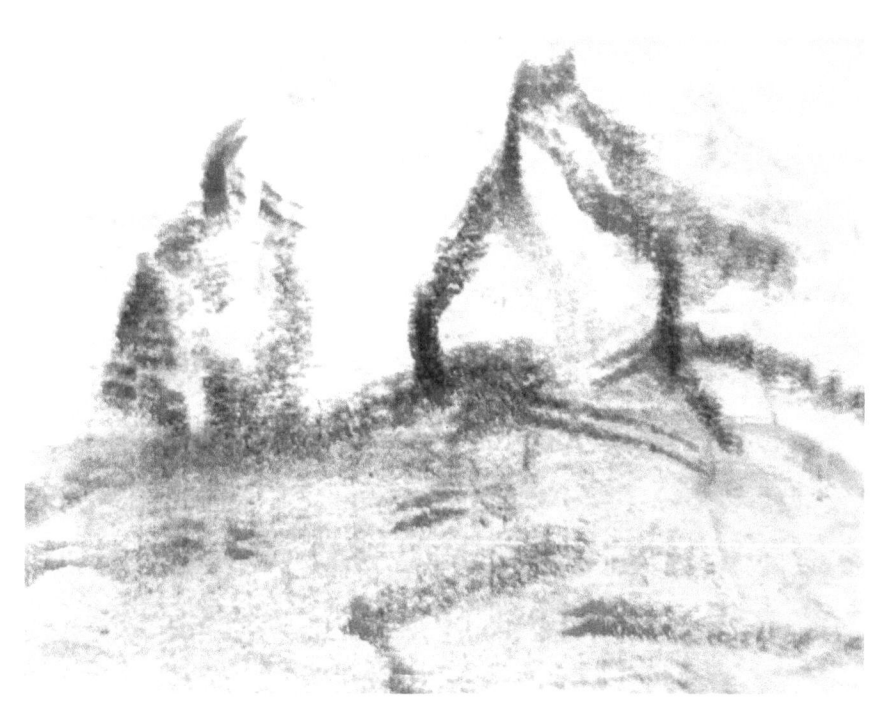

and YOU ARE WORTH IT.

beautiful,
be=you=tiful,
you

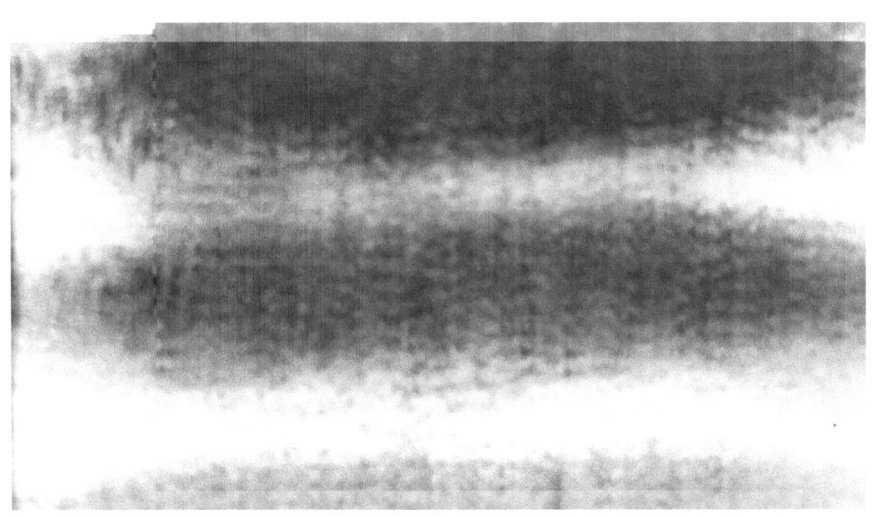

ABOUT THE AUTHOR

MILA FOX is an actress, model, makeup artist, photographer and author. In addition to acting, running her fashion blog, CHIC-ipedia, and Mila Fox Photography, Mila is an advocate for Autism Awareness and Anti-Bullying

www.ingramcontent.com/pod-product-compliance
Lightning Source LLC
Chambersburg PA
CBHW051922210526
45473CB00006B/2103